Handy Hawaii Genealogy Handbook

Gary L. Morris

©2015 Gary L. Morris

ISBN-13: 978-1507838723

ISBN-10: 1507838727

Table of Contents

Notes

Genealogical Research in Hawaii

Hawaii is the youngest American State. As such, you might think that genealogical records are rare. The opposite is actually true, and there are many historical and genealogical records available for Hawaii. Don't worry though, you won't have to dig too much for them; we'll show you exactly where they are. To get you started in tracing your Hawaii ancestry, we'll introduce you to those records, and help you to understand:

1. What they are
2. Where to find them
3. How to use them

These records can be found both online and off, so we'll introduce you to online websites, indexes and databases, as well as brick-and-mortar repositories and other institutions that will help with your research in Hawaii. So that you will have a more comprehensive understanding of these records, we have provided a brief history of the "Aloha State" to illustrate what type of records may have been generated during specific time periods. That information will assist you in pinpointing times and locations on which to focus the search for your Hawaii ancestors and their records.

A Brief History of Hawaii

Hawaii didn't become the 50th U.S. State until 1959, but its history begins many centuries ago. It is believed the first settlers were Polynesians who sailed to the islands in canoes roughly 1,500 years ago – a journey of more than 2,000 miles. Settlers from Tahiti arrived around 500 years later, and the Hawaiian culture flourished until the arrival of Captain James Cook in 1778.

Cook opened up Hawaii to the west, though he was killed within a year of his arrival. In 1791 the warring factions of the Hawaiian Islands were united by Kamehameha, and Hawaii became a unified single kingdom in 1810. In 1820, Protestant missionaries arrived and subsequently Hawaii became a thriving port for traders and whalers.

The whaling industry flourished during this time; however disease took as heavy toll on the native population. American colonists took control of the island's economy, and in 1893 they overthrew the Hawaiian Kingdom in what was a peaceful but controversial coup. Hawaii was made a U.S. Territory in 1898.

The early 20th century years saw Hawaii's economy flourish, fuelled by the large pineapple and sugar plantations. Many immigrants arrived from Portugal, the Philippines, China, and Japan, to work the plantations, and under the guidance of James Dole, Hawaii became the world's leading exporter of pineapples. On December 7, 1941 the island was rocked when the Japanese bombed Pearl Harbor, leading to the United States entering the Second World War. Hawaii became the 50th U.S. State in 1959.

Important Genealogical Dates in Hawaii History

1778 – First European contact when Captain James Cook lands at Waimea on the island of Kauai

1820 – First Protestant missionaries and whaling ships arrive

1822 – Missionaries produce first written religious text in Hawaiian

1826 – Influenza epidemic kills many native Hawaiians

1852 – Sugar plantations begin to import workers from China

1853 – Smallpox epidemic kills off large number of local population, reducing it to 75% less than in 1778 when the first Europeans arrived

1865 – Bureau of Immigration established

1875 – Hawaii grants the united States exclusive use of Pearl Harbor

1884 – Japanese immigration begins

1893 – Queen of Hawaii, Liluokalani abdicates and Hawaii changes from a kingdom to a republic

1898 – Becomes U.S. Territory

1941 – Japanese attack Pearl Harbor

1959 - Statehood

Famous Battles Fought in Hawaii

The most famous battle fought in Hawaii was the attack on Pearl Harbor during WWII. Before that however there were many battles fought between neighboring chiefs before the unification of Hawaii, and several skirmishes once it became a republic. The battle accounts can be very effective in uncovering the military records of your ancestor. They can tell you what regiments fought in which battles, and often include the names and ranks of many officers and enlisted men. Following are the most famous battles fought in Hawaii and links to useful information about them.

Battle of Moku'ohai (1782)
: http://en.wikipedia.org/wiki/Battle_of_Mokuohai

Olowalu Massacre (1790)
: http://totakeresponsibility.blogspot.de/2012/06/olowalu-massacre.html

Battle of Nu'uanu (1795):
http://www.worldhistoryblog.com/2006/04/battle-of-nuuanu.html

Battle of Diamond Head (1895), **Battle of Mo'ili'ili** (1895), **Battle of Mānoa** (1895): http://en.wikipedia.org/wiki/1895_Counter-Revolution_in_Hawaii#Battle_of_Diamond_Head

Common Hawaii Genealogical Issues and Resources to Overcome Them

Boundary Changes: Boundary changes are a common obstacle when researching Hawaii ancestors. You could be searching for an ancestor's record in one county when in fact it is stored in a different one due to historical county boundary changes. The **Atlas of Historical County Boundaries** can help you to overcome that problem. It provides a chronological listing of every boundary change that has occurred in the history of Hawaii.

Atlas of Historical County Boundaries:
http://publications.newberry.org/ahcbp/documents/HI_Consolidated
_Chronology.htm#Consolidated_Chronology

Name Changes: Surname changes, variations, and misspellings can complicate genealogical research. It is important to check all spelling variations. Soundex, a program that indexes names by sound, is a useful first step, but you can't rely on it completely as some name variations result in different Soundex codes. The surnames could be different, but the first name may be different too. You can also find records filed under initials, middle names, and nicknames as well, so you will need to **get creative with surname variations** and spellings in order to cover all the possibilities. For help with surname variations read our instructional article on **How to Use Soundex**.

get creative with surname variations:
http://obituarieshelp.org/blog/?p=634

How to Use Soundex: http://obituarieshelp.org/blog/?p=505

Hawaii Genealogical Organizations and Archives

Genealogical resources include not only records, but the organizations that house them, or can direct you to them. These institutions include: *Archives, Libraries, Genealogical Societies, Family History Centers, Universities, Churches, and Museums.*

Following are links to their websites, their physical addresses, and a summary of the records you can find there.

Hawaii Archives

Hawaii State Archives – marriage, divorce, death, probate, and naturalization records, passenger lists, military records

Iolani Palace Grounds
Honolulu, HI 96813
Telephone: 808-586-0329
Fax: 808-586-0330
Hawaii State Archives: http://archives1.dags.hawaii.gov/gsdl/cgi-bin/library?a=p&p=home&l=en&w=utf-8

National Archives at San Francisco - census records, land records, military records, passenger lists, immigration and naturalization records, Native and African American records

1000 Commodore Drive
San Bruno, CA 94066
Telephone: 415-876-9009
Fax: 415-876-9233

National Archives at San Francisco : http://www.archives.gov/san-francisco/

Hawaii State Library – wills extracts, genealogies, religious records, county records

478 South King Street
Honolulu, HI 96813
Telephone: 808-586-3500
Fax: 808-586-3584

Hawaii State Library: http://www.librarieshawaii.org/

Hawaii Chinese History Center - books, periodicals, pamphlets, photographs and genealogies, No website so only physical visitation possible.

111 North King Street Room 410
Honolulu, HI 96817
Telephone: 808-521-5948

Bishop Museum Library - books, periodicals, manuscripts, histories

1525 Bernice Street
Honolulu, HI 96817-0916
Telephone: 808-848-4148
Fax: 808-845-4133

Bishop Museum Library: http://bishopmuseumlib.lib.hawaii.edu/

University of Hawaii – ethnic records, war records, cultural histories, manuscripts, rare books

Hamilton Library, Hawaii Collection
2550 The Mall
Honolulu, HI 96822
Telephone: 808-956-7214, 808-956-7205
Fax: 808-956-5968

University of Hawaii: http://library.manoa.hawaii.edu/

Hawaii Genealogical and Historical Societies

Genealogical and historical societies have access to extensive catalogues of genealogical data. They are also able to offer expert guidance for genealogical researchers. Many members are professional genealogists who are most willing to share their expertise in finding ancestors.

Hawaiian Historical Society – journals, periodicals, manuscript collections, historical photographs, maps, histories

560 Kawaiahao Street
Honolulu, HI 96813
Telephone: 808-537-6271

Hawaiian Historical Society: http://www.hawaiianhistory.org/

Daughters of the American Revolution – library contains business records, newspapers, and Japanese-Hawaiian publications. No website for Hawaiian chapter but they do have a Facebook page.

Aloha Chapter House
1914 Makiki Heights Drive
Honolulu, HI 96822

Facebook Page: https://www.facebook.com/AlohaChapterNSDAR

Hawaii Family History Centers

The Family History Centers run by the LDS Church offer free access to billions of genealogical records for free to the general public. They also provide classes on genealogy and one-on-one assistance to inexperienced family historians. Here you will find a **Complete Listing of Hawaii Family History Centers**.

Complete Listing of Hawaii Family History Centers:
https://familysearch.org/locations/centerlocator

Additional Hawaii Genealogical Resources

Hawaii Mailing Lists

Mailing lists are internet based facilities that use email to distribute a single message to all who subscribe to it. When information on a particular surname, new records, or any other important genealogy information related to the mailing list topic becomes available, the subscribers are alerted to it. Joining a mailing list is an excellent way to stay up to date on Hawaii genealogy research topics. Rootsweb have an extensive listing of **Hawaii Mailing Lists** on a variety of topics.

Hawaii Mailing Lists:
http://lists.rootsweb.ancestry.com/index/usa/HI/misc.html

Hawaii Message Boards

A message board is another internet based facility where people can post questions about a specific genealogy topic and have it answered by other genealogists. If you have questions about a surname, record type, or research topic, you can post your question and other researchers and genealogists will help you with the answer. Be sure to check back regularly, as the answers are not emailed to you. The Hawaii message boards at **Rootsweb** are completely free to use.

Rootsweb:
http://boards.rootsweb.com/localities.northam.usa.states/mb.ashx

Hawaii Newspapers and Periodicals

Many genealogy periodicals and historical newspapers contain reprinted copies of family genealogies, transcripts of family Bible records, information about local records and archives, census indexes, church records, queries, land records, obituaries, court records, cemetery records, and wills. The following sites have historical Hawaii newspapers and periodicals that you can search online or on-site.

Hawaiian Historical Society –periodicals and historical newspaper clippings

560 Kawaiahao Street
Honolulu, HI 96813
Telephone: 808-537-6271

Hawaiian Historical Society: http://www.hawaiianhistory.org/

The Online Books Page – links to historical books and periodicals available for viewing online, dating from mid-16th century

The Online Books Page link to:
http://onlinebooks.library.upenn.edu

NewspaperArchive.com – largest online database of historical newspapers in the world.

NewspaperArchive.com: http://newspaperarchive.com/

Historical Hawaii Maps and Gazetteers

Maps are an integral part of genealogical research. They help us to locate landmarks, towns, cities, parishes, states, provinces, waterways and roads and streets. They also help us to determine when and where boundary changes might have taken place, and give us a visualization of the area we're researching in. For locating place names, a gazetteer is the best possible resource for any genealogist. Gazetteers are also sometimes called "place name dictionaries", and can help you to locate the area in which you need to conduct research. Below are links to the maps and gazetteers for research in Hawaii.

Peabody GNIS Service – Hawaii:
http://peabody.research.yale.edu/cgi-bin/Query.GNIS?ST=Hawaii&SU=1

Color Landform Atlas – Hawaii:
http://fermi.jhuapl.edu/states/hi_0.html

Hawaii Hometown Locator: http://hawaii.hometownlocator.com/

Hawaii City Directories

.

City directories are similar to telephone directories in that they list the residents of a particular area. The difference though is what is important to genealogists, and that is they pre-date telephone directories. You can find an ancestor's information such as their street address, place of employment, occupation, or the name of their spouse. A one-stop-shop for finding city directories in Hawaii is the **Hawaii Online Historical Directories** which contains a listing of every available city and historical directory related to Hawaii.

Hawaii Online Historical Directories:
https://sites.google.com/site/onlinedirectorysite/Home/usa/hi

Husted's Directory of Honolulu and Hawaiian Territory – Online access to Hawaii and Honolulu directories dating from 1880-1924.

Husted's Directory of Honolulu and Hawaiian Territory:
http://evols.library.manoa.hawaii.edu/handle/10524/12096

Hawaii Genealogical Records

<u>Birth, Death, Marriage and Divorce Records</u>

Also known as vital records, birth, death, and marriage certificates are the most basic, yet most important records attached to your ancestor. The reason for their importance is that they not only place your ancestor in a specific place at a definite time, but potentially connect the individual to other relatives. Below is a list of repositories and websites where you can find Hawaii vital records

Early Birth and Death Records

Statewide registration of births and marriages started in 1842, while the registration of deaths began in 1859. Some early birth and death records (pre-1860) were recorded by clergymen and government authorities though, and can be found at the **Hawaii State Archives**.

The **Hawaii Department of Health** has birth, marriage, divorce, and civil union records that can be ordered from the address below.

Research and Statistics Office
State Department of Health
P.O. Box 3378
1250 Punchbowl Street
Honolulu, HI 96801
Telephone: 808-586-4533

Hawaii Department of Health:
http://health.hawaii.gov/vitalrecords/

Delayed Birth Registration

Some original births in Hawaii were nit recorded and provisions were made for them to apply for a birth certificate at a later date. The **LDS Family History Centers** have these records on microfilm, and they date from 1859-1938. They also possess records that can be searched online such as:

LDS Family History Centers:
https://familysearch.org/learn/wiki/en/Category:Hawaii_Family_History_Centers

Hawaii, Births and Christenings, 1852-1933 :
https://familysearch.org/search/collection/1674805

Hawaii, Marriages, 1826-1922:
https://familysearch.org/search/collection/1674811

Hawaii Deaths and Burials, 1862-1919:
https://familysearch.org/search/collection/1674810

Census Reports

Census records are among the most important genealogical documents for placing your ancestor in a particular place at a specific time. Like BDM records, they can also lead you to other ancestors, particularly those who were living under the authority of the head of household.

Censuses were taken in Hawaii between the years of the federal censuses, and the 1878, 1890, and 1896 records can be found at the **Hawaii State Archives**. Official Federal Census records are available from 1900-1940, and indexes can be searched online at **Family Search**.

Hawaii State Archives: http://ags.hawaii.gov/archives/about-us/genealogy-research-guide/census-records/

Family Search: https://familysearch.org/

Access Genealogy also has Hawaii census records from 1900-1940 that can be viewed online.

Access Genealogy:
http://www.accessgenealogy.com/census/hawaii-census-records.htm

Hawaii Church Records

Church and synagogue records are a valuable resource, especially for baptisms, marriages, and burials that took place before 1900. You will need to at least have an idea of your ancestor's religious denomination, and in most cases you will have to visit a brick and mortar establishment to view them.

Most church records are kept by the individual church, although in some denominations, records are placed in a regional archive or maintained at the diocesan level. Local Historical Societies are sometimes the repository for the state's older church records. In Hawaii many of the Vital Records from Churches are held in the state archives. Below are links archives that maintain church records, as well as a few databases that can be viewed online.

The **Family History Library** contains many church records from a variety of denominations on microfilm.

Family History Library:
http://familysearch.org/learn/wiki/en/Family_History_Library

Hawaii State Archives – marriage, divorce, death, probate, and naturalization records, passenger lists, military records

Hawaii State Archives: http://archives1.dags.hawaii.gov/gsdl/cgi-bin/library?a=p&p=home&l=en&w=utf-8

On the following pages you will find details of Central repositories for Denominational records that you can request copies of Baptism, Marriage, and other church related records.

Central Repositories for Denominational Records

Most of the records of individual denominations are kept in central repositories. Below is a list of the major congregational archives in Hawaii with links to their websites, physical addresses, and contact information.

Congregational

Congregational Library
14 Beacon Street
Boston, MA 02108
Telephone: 617-523-0470
Fax: 617-523-0470

Congregational: http://www.14beacon.org/

Presbyterian

Presbyterian Historical Society
425 Lombard Street
Philadelphia, PA 19147-1516
Telephone: 215-627-1852
Fax: 215-627-0509

Presbyterian: http://www.history.pcusa.org/

Roman Catholic

Diocese of Honolulu, Chancery Office
1184 Bishop Street
Honolulu, HI 96813
Telephone: 808-533-1791
Fax: 808-521-8428

Roman Catholic: http://www.catholichawaii.org/

Buddhist records are held by the individual Buddhist temples.

Buddhist;
http://www.yelp.com/search?cflt=buddhist_temples&find_loc=Hono
lulu%2C+HI

Hawaii Military Records

More than 40 million Americans have participated in some time of war service since America was colonized. The chance of finding your ancestor amongst those records is exceptionally high. Military records can even reveal individuals who never actually served, such as those who registered for the two World Wars but were never called to duty.

Below are a number of links to websites and archives that contain Hawaii military records.

U.S. National Archives – WWI Draft registration cards, casualties lists, WWI and WWII service records, Korean War records, Vietnam War records, Civil War and Spanish-American War records, and casualties lists.

U.S. National Archives:
http://www.archives.gov/research/military/veterans/online.html

US Department of Veterans Affairs Nationwide Gravesite Locator – includes information on veterans and their family members buried in veterans and military cemeteries having a government grave marker.

US Department of Veterans Affairs Nationwide Gravesite Locator: http://gravelocator.cem.va.gov/

Hawaii Cemetery Records

As convenient as it is to search cemetery records online, keep in mind that there are a few disadvantages over visiting a cemetery in person. They are:

- Tombstone information is not always accurately transcribed
- The arrangement of the graves in a cemetery can be crucial as family members are often buried next to each other or in the same grave. This arrangement is not always preserved in the alphabetical indexes that are found online.

With that information in mind, the following websites have databases that can be searched online for Hawaii Cemetery records.

Hawaii Tombstone Transcription Project - death and burial records

Hawaii Tombstone Transcription Project:
http://www.usgwtombstones.org/hawaii/hawaii.html

Find a Grave – over 100 million grave records can be searched on this site. Search can be conducted by name, location, or cemetery name.

Find a Grave: http://www.findagrave.com/

Interment.net - A free online database containing approximately 4 million cemetery records from around the world.

Interment.net: http://www.interment.net/

Billion Graves – as the name implies, you can search a billion records including headstone photos, transcriptions, cemetery records, and grave locations.

Billion Graves:
http://billiongraves.com/pages/search/index.php#cemetery

Hawaii Obituaries

Obituaries can reveal a wealth about our ancestor and other relatives. You can search our **Hawaii Newspaper Obituaries Listings** from hundreds of Hawaii newspapers online for free.

Hawaii Newspaper Obituaries Listings:
http://obituarieshelp.org/hawaii_newspaper_obituaries.html

Hawaii Wills and Probate Records

The documents found in a probate packet may include a complete inventory of a person's estate, newspaper entries, witness testimony, a copy of a will, list of debtors and creditors, names of executors or trustees, names of heirs. They can not only tell you about the ancestor you're currently researching, but lead to other ancestors. Most of these records must be accessed at a county court or clerk's office, but some can be found online as well. You can obtain copies of the original probate records by writing to the county clerk.

Additionally **The State Archives of Hawaii** and the **Family History Centers** have 141 microfilms of indexes from 1814 to 1917 and probate records from 1845 to 1900. Original records can be found at individual county courthouses.

The State Archives of Hawaii:
http://archives1.dags.hawaii.gov/gsdl/cgi-bin/library?a=p&p=home&l=en&w=utf-8

Family History Library:
https://familysearch.org/learn/wiki/en/Category:Hawaii_Family_History_Centers

Hawaii Immigration and Naturalization Records

The naturalization process generated many types of records, including petitions, declarations of intention, and oaths of allegiance. These records can provide family historians with information such as a person's birth date and place of birth, immigration year, marital status, spouse information, occupation, witnesses' names and addresses, and more.

The **Hawaii State Archives** have passenger lists for Japanese, Chinese, and Portuguese immigrants containing almost 50,000 records, and naturalization records from1874 to 1904 and petitions from 1900 and 1904.

Hawaii State Archives: http://archives1.dags.hawaii.gov/gsdl/cgi-bin/library?a=p&p=home&l=en&w=utf-8

US National Archives – Immigration and Naturalization records for the entire United States

US National Archives:
http://www.archives.gov/research/immigration/passenger-arrival.html

Native Hawaiian Records

Native Hawaiian records can be difficult to locate, but there are available sources of them. Below are the best resources for tracing native Hawaiian ancestry.

Manoa Library – University of Hawaii:
http://guides.library.manoa.hawaii.edu/content.php?pid=143954&sid=1243293

Office of Hawaiian Affairs: http://www.oha.org/page/genealogy-help

Hawaiian Roots : http://www.hawaiian-roots.com/

Hawaii Genweb:
http://www.rootsweb.ancestry.com/~higenweb/hawaii.htm

Missing Matriarchs – Resources for Researching Female Hawaii Ancestors

Looking for female ancestors requires an adjustment of how we view traditional records sources. A woman's identity was often under that of her husband, and often individual records for them can be difficult to locate. The following resources are effective in locating female ancestors in Hawaii where traditional records may not reveal them.

Marriage and Divorce Records

The earliest Hawaiian marriage records date from the early 1800's. Marriage and divorce records for the kingdom began in 1853, and in 1884, lists were submitted on a quarterly basis. The majority of records prior to 1896 are at the State Archives, while those produced after 1896 are at the Department of Health. Other records have been filmed as follows:

1. Marriage records 1826-1929 (film 1031145), marriage records 1909-1920 (film 1851162 ff.), and Index to the Archives of Hawaii (film 1031145) at the **Bernice P. Bishop Museum** in Honolulu.
2. Kingdom of Hawaii marriage records for Maui, Molokai, Oahu, and Kauai, 1884-1896 (film 1205810 ff.) and Territory of Hawaii marriage records, 1904-1909 (film 195531 ff.) at the **Department of Health** in Honolulu
3. Marriage records 1800-1850 (index on film 1031144) at the **Daughters of the American Revolution Memorial Library** in Honolulu
4. Early Congregational Church records from 1820 at the **Hawaiian Mission Children's Society Library** in Honolulu
5. Index to marriages listed in Hawaiian newspapers prior to 1950 (film 1002822) and marriage extracts from newspapers 1862-1909 (film 1675269 ff.) at the **Genealogical Service Center** in Honolulu

Bibliographies

- *Genealogical Sources in Hawaii,* Agnes C. Conrad (Honolulu Library Association, 1987)
- *Paths of Duty: American Missionary Wives in Nineteenth Century Hawaii,* Patricia Grimshaw (Honolulu University Press, 1989)
- *Women's Voices in Hawaii,* Joyce Chapman Lebra (University Press of Colorado, 1991)
- *Japanese Women in Hawaii: The First 100 Years,* Patsy S. Saki (Kisaku, 1985)
- *The Chinese in Hawaii: An Annotated Bibliography,* Nancy Foon Young (University of Hawaii Press, 1973)

Selected Resources for Hawaii Women's History

D.A.R Memorial Library
1914 Makiki Heights Drive
Honolulu, HI 96822

Daughters of Hawaii
2913 Pali Highway
Honolulu, HI 96817

Bernice Pauahi Bishop Museum Library
1525 Bernice St.
PO Box 19000-A
Honolulu, HI 96817-0916

Common Hawaii Surnames

The following surnames are among the most common in Hawaii and are also being currently researched by other genealogists. If you find your surname here, there is a chance that some research has already been performed on your ancestor.

Akana, Akina, Akuini, Alapai, Allen, Amalu, Among, Amoy, Aneko, Ano, Awana, Bactio, Balderston, Balino, Bell, Bertelmann, Branco, Carminati, Chang, Choy, Coiner, Coney, Conway, Crowell, Cruz, Feary, Fern, Forsyth, Freitas, Fun, George, Gomes, Gray, Gutierres, Haiku, Hailama, Hamilton, Hiram, Hoapili, Hoke, Hookano, Iaukea, Jesus, Jordan, Kaai, Kaanaana, Kaapana, Kahaulelio, Kahike, Kahiona, Kahoiwai, Kaialiilii, Kailikea, Kaiuwaihui, Kalainawai, Kalakona, Kalani, Kalei, Kalima, Kaoao, Kapahu, Kawaha, Keao, Keaunui, Keawe, Keaweamahi, Kekahuna, Kekumu, Keone, Kiliona, Lachance, Lane, Lee, Lehman, Lincoln, Liwai, Londeree, Lono, Lonoehu, Look, Luahoomae, Mahaulu, Manunui, Mika, Miranda, Moi, Moliakalaniikeola, Mossman, Naihe, Nakanaela, Natua, Nawahine, Needham, Newalu, Onakea, Paahao, Pahia, Paikuli, Palea, Paradis, Pi, Pookalani, PuhihaleE, Richard, Robert, Sales, Salias, Seabury, Senna, Silva, Smith, Stiehl, Victor, Wahine, Wardlaw, Whitmarsh, Wilson, Wong, Wood

About the Author

Gary L. Morris worked from 2009 to 2014 as a professional researcher for a major player in the genealogy field. After tracing his family lineage back to 1683, he found that genealogy could be an expensive undertaking. As such, has decided to publish these helpful guides to share the valuable free information he has discovered during his career to help others trace their family lineages as inexpensively as possible. An avid genealogist himself, he hopes you will find this guide factual, thorough, helpful, and most of all, effective in helping you to find your family members.

Notes

Notes

www.ingramcontent.com/pod-product-compliance
Lightning Source LLC
Chambersburg PA
CBHW070526290526
45790CB00003B/1309